Pizza at

Writ
Illustrate

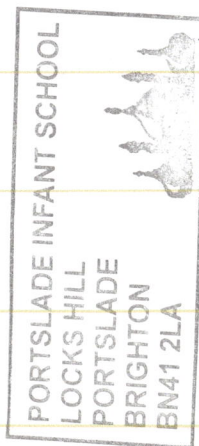

Published by Pearson Education Limited, Edinburgh Gate, Harlow, Essex, CM20 2JE
Registered company number: 872828

www.pearsonschools.co.uk

Text © Dominic Barker 2011

Designed by Bigtop
Original illustrations © Pearson Education 2011
Illustrated by Paule Trudel Bellemare

The right of Dominic Barker to be identified as author of this work has been asserted by him in
accordance with the Copyright, Designs and Patents Act 1988.

First published 2011

15 14 13 12 11
10 9 8 7 6 5 4 3 2 1

British Library Cataloguing in Publication Data
A catalogue record for this book is available from the British Library

ISBN 978 0 435 91518 6

Printed and bound at Ashford Colour Press

Acknowledgements
We would like to thank the children and teachers of Bangor Central Primary School, NI;
Bishop Henderson C of E Primary School, Somerset; Brookside Community Primary School,
Somerset; Cheddington Combined School, Buckinghamshire; Cofton Primary School,
Birmingham; Dair House Independent School, Buckinghamshire; Newbold Riverside Primary
School, Rugby and Windmill Primary School, Oxford for their invaluable help in the
development and trialling of the Bug Club resources.

Every effort has been made to contact copyright holders of material reproduced in this book.
Any omissions will be rectified in subsequent printings if notice is given to the publishers.

CHAPTER 1

I Like Pizza!

"It's Saturday," said Mum to Jack, "so you get to pick what we have for tea. What's it going to be?"

"Pizza," said Jack instantly.

"Pizza?" repeated his mum. "You always pick pizza. You need to vary your diet. You could pick pasta or curry or ..."

"Pizza," Jack assured her.

"Chilli?"

"Pizza."

Every Saturday his mum tried to get him to pick something different.

The doorbell rang. Jack ran to answer.

"Hey Shaz," he said, pleased to see his best friend. "What's happ..."

He stopped.

"What's he doing here?"

The 'he' was a boy called Oliver. He had moved in over the road and had one very unusual thing about him – he looked exactly like Jack.

"Don't you remember what happened last time we hung out with him?" Jack asked angrily.

Jack remembered. He'd ended up trapped in another school with everybody shouting at him because they thought he was Oliver.

"He's very sorry about that," explained Shazia. "My mum says Oliver was probably upset by moving house." Shazia's mum was a doctor.

"Upset by the move," agreed Oliver, casually shaking a can of cola. "Very common."

"So we've got to give him another chance," said Shazia.

Jack looked at Oliver warily.

"No more pretending to be me," he said.

"Course not," said Oliver. "Even if I wanted to I couldn't because you're wearing a red t-shirt and I'm wearing a blue one."

"Please, boys!" urged Shazia.

Jack looked at Shazia. Once she'd made up her mind to do something, nothing was ever going to change it.

"OK," he sighed.

Shazia smiled.

"I'm going out, Mum," Jack shouted.

"OK," shouted back his mum. "Remember to be back in time for your favourite pizza."

"I like pizza!" said Oliver.

"Try Jack's mum's," advised Shazia. "It's the best pizza in the world."

Oliver licked his lips.

CHAPTER 2

Ooops!

"What are we going to do?" asked Shazia.

"First, I've got to go to my gran's for a bit," Oliver said. "It's her birthday. My dad said I've got to take a card round to her. You could come with me. It's not far. Then we can hang out."

Jack looked doubtful. But Shazia was keen.

"Of course we'll come with you," she said. "That's what friends are for."

"Thanks," said Oliver. "Do you want a swig of cola?"

He pulled back the ring pull.

The can exploded all over him.

"Ooops!" he said.

"Why were you shaking it?" asked Jack. "It was bound to do that."

"I wasn't thinking," agreed Oliver. "I'd better go and change."

He went over to his house. Two minutes later he was back, wearing a red t-shirt.

"Exactly the same clothes as me," said Jack.

"What a coincidence," said Oliver.

CHAPTER 3

Who Is It?

"Happy Birthday, Gran!"

"Who is it?" asked the old lady peering at them from the doorway.

"Oliver!"

"Oliver who? I haven't got my glasses on."

"Oliver, your grandson."

"Oh! That Oliver," said Gran.

"I've brought two of my friends to meet you," said Oliver. "This is Shaz and this is Jack."

"You're all a blur to me," said Gran. "You'd better come in and have some tea. Oliver, your dad phoned to say he'd be coming round soon with a cake."

"I thought we were just going to say hello," whispered Jack.

"We have to go in," hissed Shazia. "We've been invited. And what could possibly happen in an old lady's house?"

CHAPTER 4

A New Me

"Don't mind Mr Tiddles," said Gran as a large tabby cat jumped off the back of the sofa onto Jack. "He's only playing."

Mr Tiddles gave Jack a mean stare and sank his claws into his leg.

"Ow!" cried Jack.

"Where did I put my glasses?" asked Gran. "It would be so nice to look at you young people properly. Can anybody see them?"

They looked around the room. Every shelf was crammed with trinkets and ornaments, but no glasses.

"I don't think they're here," said Shazia.

"Perhaps I left them in my bedroom," said Gran. "As soon as I've found them I'll pop the kettle on."

"Gran," said Oliver sweetly, putting a birthday card on the mantelpiece. "Have you got any chores that I could do while you're looking?"

Gran looked puzzled.

"You don't normally offer to do chores, Oliver."

"You're seeing a new me," he explained.

"Well ... the washing-up needs doing."

Gran went to find her glasses.

Oliver stood up to go to do the washing-up.

"Ooops!" he said. "I forgot about my watch!"

"What about it?" asked Shazia.

"I'm not sure it's waterproof," said Oliver. "So, take it off now and put it back on when you've finished," said Jack, sounding puzzled.

"Bad idea. Every time I've done

that before, I've forgotten it. Be a
mate, Jack, and wear it for me. Then
I can't forget it."

"Er ..." said Jack doubtfully.

"You can give it right back as
soon as I've finished," insisted Oliver.
"It's just so I won't forget it. My
dad got it as a present from Japan.
It's rare and he went crazy the last
time he thought I'd lost it. Go on."

Oliver held out the watch.

Jack hesitated.

"I could wear it,"
suggested Shazia.

"It's a boy's watch,"
said Oliver, firmly.

"You aren't scared of
a watch, are you Jack?"

Jack saw Shazia looking at him.

"Course not," he said, taking it.

Oliver grinned.

CHAPTER 5

Don't Play Games!

"I found them!" said Gran, putting on her glasses. "Oh I am excited," she said to herself. "This is the first time Oliver's ever bought me a card."

"Wouldn't you prefer to open it when Oliver's here?" suggested Shazia. "Where is he, anyway?" she asked, looking around.

Gran gave her a hard stare.

"Oliver's here!" she said, indicating Jack and then tearing open the envelope and pulling out her card.

Shazia and Jack exchanged glances. This was a little embarrassing.

"I think ..." began Shazia.

But she was interrupted by Gran reading out her card.

Dear Gran

Happy Birthday! Because I love you so much, today I will do all your chores. I'll wash the dishes, mow the lawn, tidy the house, vacuum all the carpets and even shampoo Mr Tiddles.

Love,
Oliver xx

Oliver's gran gave Jack a sweet smile.

"You really have changed, Oliver."

"This isn't Oliver," explained Shazia.

"Of course he's Oliver."

"I'm not," said Jack.

"Are you saying I don't know my own grandson?"

"No, no," said Shazia. "It's just that Oliver looks like Jack."

"Oh, your friend Jack," said Oliver's gran. "He's gone."

"What?" said Jack and Shazia together.

"He said to tell you he got an urgent text, whatever that is, and he had to go. He'll see you later."

"But didn't you see that Jack who isn't the real Jack looked exactly like Oliver?" asked Shazia.

"Don't play games with me!" said Gran. "Now, Oliver. About those chores …"

The two children looked at each other in horror.

Oliver had done it again …

CHAPTER 6

Tricked Again!

"There really has been a horrible misunderstanding," said Shazia. "We're going to have to go."

"You can go whenever you like," said Gran. "But Oliver here has got to do the chores he promised."

"But I'm not Oliver," said Jack.

"We'll go and find the real

Oliver," promised Shazia, "and tell him that he's got to do your chores."

But before they could leave they heard the front door bang. Oliver's dad strode into the room carrying a large cake.

"Happy Birthday, Dear Mum!" he sang.

He plonked the cake down.

"Glad to see you're already here, Oliver," he said. "And you've brought a friend – how nice."

Jack and Shazia exchanged desperate glances. The similarity between the two boys was so striking that even their parents couldn't tell them apart.

"Er, I'm not Oliver," said Jack.

"No he's not," said Shazia.

"They keep saying that," said Gran. "I think Oliver's trying to get out of doing the chores."

"What do you mean?" asked Oliver's dad.

Gran showed him the birthday card.

"Well, well," said Oliver's dad, "if Oliver promised to do all those chores then he will do them. Won't you, Oliver?"

"But I'm not Oliver. I'm Jack!"

Oliver's dad began to look annoyed.

"I have heard enough of this 'I want to change my name' nonsense. All week you've been saying 'I'm sick of being called Oliver. I want to change my name to Jack. Jack's a better name.' Your name is, always has been and always will be – OLIVER!'

Shazia and Jack groaned.

"He's tricked us again!"

"What's that?" said Gran.

Shazia tried to explain. "I promise you, this isn't Oliver."

"And who are YOU?" demanded Oliver's dad.

"I'm Shazia. And I'm a register monitor. So you must believe me."

There was a moment of silence. Shazia had spoken so confidently that maybe they might believe her. But ...

"If this isn't Oliver," said Oliver's dad suddenly, "why is he wearing Oliver's watch?"

"Er ..." said Jack.

"Er ..." echoed Shaz.

"Aha! Got you!" said Oliver's dad, pointing at Shazia. "Now stop your games and go home. Oliver has got some chores to do."

Shazia and Jack looked helplessly at one another. Jack was stuck with being Oliver again. And who knew what Oliver was up to, now that he was Jack?

CHAPTER 7

Get That Paddling Pool

"According to this birthday card you've still got one more chore to go. Your gran has gone for her afternoon nap and I want the last job completed by the time she wakes up."

So far, under Oliver's dad's watchful eye, Jack had washed up, tidied the house, vacuumed the carpets and mowed the lawn. There hadn't been a moment when he'd been able to get away. Now only one chore remained. The most daunting of all: washing Mr Tiddles!

"Get the old paddling pool out of the garage," said Oliver's dad. "We know Mr Tiddles doesn't like being washed so it's better to do it outside."

Jack headed for the garage. He felt his phone vibrate.

> ✉ **1 new message!**
> **Oliver at your house. Says he's going to eat your pizza! Sorry! Shaz**

His favourite pizza! He'd forgotten all about it. And now Oliver was going to get to eat it. No way! He had to stop him.

There had to be a way to escape without Oliver's dad seeing him.

He slipped down the side of the garage, trying to avoid the nettles. Yes! He just needed to get past the garage and ...

"Where do you think you're going?"

Oliver's dad had followed him. Jack remembered that this was the problem with being Oliver – everybody was always expecting the worst of him so you could never get away with anything.

"But I didn't think you needed to bath cats," said Jack, desperately trying to find an excuse to get away.

"You know very well the vet says that Mr Tiddles needs to be washed with a special shampoo sometimes," said Oliver's dad crossly. "Now hurry up and get that paddling pool. I'll fill it with water and you find Mr Tiddles."

CHAPTER 8

There's A Nice Puss-cat

Mr Tiddles was not a big fan of baths. As soon he as saw the water he started squirming and struggling in Jack's arms.

"Don't let go of him!" ordered Oliver's dad.

Easier said than done. Just as Jack began to lower Mr Tiddles into the paddling pool, the cat leaped from his arms and climbed straight up the nearby tree.

"I told you not to let him go!"

"I couldn't help it." Mr Tiddles sat just out of reach, glaring and hissing at them.

Oliver's dad wasn't happy.

"We'll have to get him out of that tree," he said. "If I lift you up quickly, you can reach up and grab him."

Jack looked up at Mr Tiddles, who was still looking down at them with hate in his eyes and hissing. He really didn't want to ...

But it was too late.

"I don't even like cats," thought Jack as Oliver's dad lifted him onto his shoulders.

"There's a nice puss-cat," said Jack, hopefully.

Flattery was not working with Mr Tiddles.

The moment Jack reached for him, he swiped a paw angrily at him and ran further up the tree.

"Whoah!" cried Jack as he reeled backwards and desperately tried to keep his balance. He swayed backwards and forwards as Oliver's dad stumbled around under him.

Then Jack felt himself flying through the air and landing on the grass with a thud. When he looked up he saw it wasn't Mr Tiddles who was having a bath – it was Oliver's dad.

"Aaargh!" he shouted from the paddling pool. "I've got shampoo in my eyes ..."

"Uh, oh!" thought Jack. "Time to run!"

CHAPTER 9

That's MY Tea!

Jack ran all the way home and found Shazia waiting for him.

"Where have you been?" she demanded.

"It's a long story," said Jack. "But Oliver's in BIG trouble. I've got to get back to being Jack."

"That's not going to be easy," said Shazia. "Look!"

Jack looked through the window and saw that Oliver was sitting in his place at the dinner table. Even Jack's mother hadn't recognised that Oliver was a different boy.

"What can we do to show he's not the real you?" asked Shazia.

Before Jack could answer, they heard a car pull up sharply. Oliver's dad!

"Come on!" said Jack.

He and Shazia ran straight into the house.

Oliver looked up as they came in. He seemed very surprised.

"What do you think you're doing?" demanded Jack.

But Oliver ignored him.

"Mum, Shaz and that boy from over the road have just come into the house without being asked," he shouted.

Jack's mum appeared from the kitchen carrying a pizza.

"Mum!" said Jack.

"Don't call my mum 'Mum'," said Oliver.

"She's not *your* mum, she's *my* mum."

Jack couldn't believe that Oliver was even trying to steal his mum!

There was a loud knock at the door. Mum answered and Oliver's dad marched in, looking furious. He stared straight at Jack.

"Oliver. Get home now!"

"I'm not Oliver."

"Yes he is," said Oliver from the table.

"No, he's not," said Shazia.

"What on earth is going on here?" demanded Jack's mum, putting the pizza on the table.

"That's what I want to know," said Oliver's dad. "One of these two is my son and whichever one it is in BIG trouble."

"I just want to eat my pizza in peace," said Oliver smugly, picking up a slice and biting into it.

Seeing Oliver sitting at *his* table eating *his* pizza was more than Jack could bear.

"That's MY tea," he said, grabbing a slice and biting into it. "Uuurgh!" he said. "That's horrible!"

"That settles it," said Oliver's dad staring angrily at Jack. "You're so rude you must be Oliver. Come with me NOW!"

"Wait a minute," said Jack's mum. She turned to Oliver, sitting at the table.

"Do you think this pizza is nice?" she asked.

"Yes, Mummy," said Oliver sweetly. "Everyone says you make the best pizza."

"And," she said turning to Jack, "you think it's horrible."

"Yes," he said. "It's got anchovies on it."

"I think I can say who the real Oliver is," announced Jack's mum.

Everyone looked at her. There was a tense silence.

"You see," she explained. "Jack always wants pizza for his Saturday tea and I keep trying to get him to eat different things. So to make sure he picked something else next time I put anchovies on today's pizza – he hates them! Which means the boy who does like this pizza must be Oliver."

All eyes turned to the real Oliver. "Did I say it was nice? ... I meant nasty ... Yuck ... It was disgusting ... I want to be sick ... I ..."

But it was too late. Oliver had been caught. "You've got a lot of explaining to do," said his dad.

And then he turned to Jack.

"I owe you an apology," he said.

"And me," said Shazia, who didn't want to miss out.

"I'm sorry," he said to both of them. "But if it makes you feel any better, Oliver's gran was so pleased with all the chores you did that she asked me to give you this twenty-pound note."

Jack gasped with pleasure. Oliver looked as if he were about to explode.

Oliver's dad handed over the money to Jack and then turned to his own son.

"Now you, Oliver, have a cat to shampoo. Come on!"

"Not Mr Tiddles!" protested Oliver in horror.

But there was no escape. Oliver was led away to his soapy fate.

Jack's mum turned to Jack and Shazia.

"I am glad to have my own son back," she said. "And to celebrate, I'm going to make him the biggest and the best pizza he's ever tasted."

"Yes!" shouted Jack.

"In fact, it's going to be so big that he'll probably need a friend to help him eat it."

Jack and Shazia burst out laughing.

"Pizza at the double!"